PUFFIN BOOKS

What Goes Up White & Comes Down Yellow?

What Goes Up White & Comes Down Yellow?

Gyles Brandreth

PUFFIN

PUFFIN BOOKS

UK | USA | Canada | Ireland | Australia
India | New Zealand | South Africa

Puffin Books is part of the Penguin Random House group of companies
whose addresses can be found at global.penguinrandomhouse.com.

www.penguin.co.uk   www.puffin.co.uk   www.ladybird.co.uk

First published 2022

001

Text copyright © Gyles Brandreth, 2022
Illustrations copyright © Emily Fox, 2022

The moral right of the author and illustrator has been asserted

Text design by Dan Newman and Sally Griffin

The authorized representative in the EEA is Penguin Random House Ireland,
Morrison Chambers, 32 Nassau Street, Dublin D02 YH68

Printed in Great Britain by Clays Ltd, Elcograf S.p.A

A CIP catalogue record for this book is available from the British Library

ISBN: 978-0-241-54447-1

All correspondence to:
Puffin Books, Penguin Random House Children's
One Embassy Gardens, 8 Viaduct Gardens
London, SW11 7BW

Dedicated to
KITT
ATTICUS
CORNELIUS
CASSIAN
ISOLDE
RORY
KIYO

CONTENTS

CHAPTER 1

HELLO!

When first I **APPEAR** I seem **mysterious**,

But when I am **EXPLAINED**

I am nothing **serious**.

WHAT AM I?

A RIDDLE,

OF COURSE!

WHAT IS A RIDDLE?

It is a **QUESTION** that has a CLEVER, SURPRISING or FUNNY **ANSWER**. Every riddle is a kind of **PUZZLE** and a lot of riddles are **JOKES** as well – and a lot of jokes are **RIDDLES**!

How do I know?
Because I am **GYLES BRANDRETH**, MASTER OF FUNNY and COLLECTOR OF RIDDLES. I have been **RIDDLE-GATHERING** for as long as I can remember.

The **FIRST RIDDLE** I ever heard is still one of my **FAVOURITES**:

What gets wetter the more it DRIES?

⭐ **ANSWER:** *A towel. Do you get it? The more a towel dries you, the wetter the towel gets.*

The **OLDEST RIDDLE** I know is the **RIDDLE OF THE SPHINX**. It is **THOUSANDS** of years old and comes to us from ancient Greece. According to legend, the sphinx was a terrifying monster with the FACE OF A HUMAN, the BODY OF A LION and the WINGS OF A BIRD. Everyone who passed the SPHINX was asked the **RIDDLE**, and, if they could not answer it, they were killed:

What is it that goes on four legs in the MORNING,
Two legs at NOON,
And three legs in the EVENING?

To **SAVE** your life, can you **UNRAVEL** the riddle?

3

⭐ **ANSWER:** *A human being. Why? Because in the morning of our lives, when we're babies, we crawl on all fours. In the middle of our lives, at noon, we walk on two legs. And in the evening of our lives, when we are old, we use a walking stick, giving us three legs.*

Riddles come in all shapes and sizes. Some are **SHORT**:

No sooner spoken than broken – WHAT IS IT?

⭐ **ANSWER:** *Silence. (When you speak, you are 'breaking the silence'!)*

Some are **LONG**:

You are on a journey with a **fox**, a **goose** and a **sack of corn**. You come to a stream that you have to cross, and you find a small boat you can use to do so. The **PROBLEM** is that the size of the boat means you can only take yourself and either the fox, the goose or the corn across at one time. It is not possible to leave the fox alone with the goose, or the goose alone with the corn, because if you do the fox will eat the goose, or the goose will eat the corn. How can you get the **fox**, the **goose** and the **corn** all safely over the stream?

ANSWER: *Take the goose over first and come back. Next take the fox over, then bring the goose back. Now take the corn over and come back alone to get the goose. Take the goose over and the job is done!*

Some are **ANCIENT**:

I have a tail, and I have a head,

but I have no body. I am not a snake.

WHAT AM I?

 ANSWER: *A coin.*

Some are **MODERN**:

Three eyes have I, all in a row;

When the red one opens, everything STOPS.

WHAT AM I?

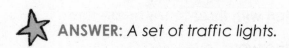 ANSWER: *A set of traffic lights.*

Some riddles are **SERIOUS** and need THINKING through:

PRONOUNCED as one letter,

And WRITTEN with three,

Two letters there are,

And two only in me.

I'm double, I'm single,

I'm black, blue and grey,

I'm read from both ends,

And the same either way.

WHAT AM I?

 ANSWER: *An eye.*

Did you work it out?

The clues are all there:

- **'Pronounced as one letter'** – like the ninth letter of the alphabet, the letter 'I'.

- **'And written with three'** – there are three letters in the word 'eye'.

- **'Two letters there are'** – an 'E' and a 'Y'.

- **'And two only in me'** – you have two eyes in your head.

- **'I'm double, I'm single'** – you have a pair of eyes, but each one is individual.

- **'I'm black, blue and grey'** – three of the colours eyes can be.

- **'I'm read from both ends, and the same either way'** – you can read the word 'eye' either forward or backwards.

It's CLEVER stuff, eh? Aye, aye! (That's clever stuff, too: 'aye' is an old word for 'yes'.)

'AYE' and **'EYE'** and **'I'** all sound the same. Words that sound the same but have different meanings are called **HOMOPHONES**. Homophones often pop up in PUNS. A pun is a fun way to use a word or phrase to give it more than one meaning – for example:

What did the waiter say to the customer who complained that the EGGS he had just been served tasted DISGUSTING?

'Don't blame me – I only laid the table!'

Get it?

Hens lay eggs and people lay tables. 'Lay' is one word, but it has several meanings.

Shall we have salad for LUNCH?

Yes, lettuce!

Get it?

'Lettuce' and 'let us' sound the same. Lots of
SILLY RIDDLES involve puns, but not all of them
do. And even the silliest riddles may need
careful THINKING THROUGH, too.

What goes ninety-nine BONK?

A centipede with a wooden leg.

Get it?

The word 'centipede' comes from Latin, an
old language in which **'CENTUM'** means a
hundred and **'PEDIS'** means foot, so the name
suggests centipedes should have one hundred
feet. In fact, despite their name, centipedes do
not have one hundred feet. Centipedes can
have a varying number of legs, ranging from

thirty to 354. The legs of centipedes come in pairs and every centipede has an odd number of pairs of legs, so no centipede ever has exactly one hundred legs. It is a **VERY SILLY RIDDLE**.

With some riddles, there is more than one possible answer. If I said to you, 'What's black and white and red all over?' what would you say? You might say, 'Gyles, it's the title of my **FAVOURITE** book!' And, if you did, I'd be delighted because I have written a book called *What's Black and White and Red All Over?* It's a joke book. In fact, it is the **BEST WORST** joke book in the world and it is published by Puffin, of course. I decided to call it *What's Black and White and Red All Over?* because that's a riddling question with several possible answers – each one, I think, **SILLIER** and **FUNNIER** than the last.

What's **BLACK** and **WHITE** and **RED ALL OVER**?

A newspaper.

What's **BLACK** and **WHITE** and **RED ALL OVER**?

A sunburnt zebra.

What's **BLACK** and **WHITE** and **RED ALL OVER**?

An embarrassed penguin.

What's **BLACK** and **WHITE** and **RED ALL OVER**?

A skunk with nappy rash.

What's **BLACK** and **WHITE** and **RED ALL OVER**?

A chocolate sundae
with tomato ketchup all over it.

There are at least **THREE** possible answers

to this famous riddle:

What goes over the water,
And under the water,
But doesn't touch the water?

 The **ANSWER** could be:

1. *A ray of sunshine.*

2. *A duck's egg tucked inside a mother duck.*

3. *A person crossing a bridge over a river or a*
stream, carrying a pail of water on their head.

And I can think of at least two answers to this one:

What is EASY to get into but HARD to get out of?

Depending on how naughty you are – or how

lazy – the **ANSWER** could be either *trouble* or *bed*.

As soon as you know the answer to a riddle, it seems OBVIOUS. For example, the old nursery rhyme about Humpty Dumpty is really a riddle:

Humpty Dumpty SAT on a wall,
Humpty Dumpty had a GREAT fall.
All the king's horses and all the king's men,
Couldn't put Humpty together again.

WHO or WHAT is Humpty Dumpty?

Because you ALREADY know that Humpty Dumpty is an egg, the riddle seems very easy.

Here's another old nursery-rhyme riddle that WON'T seem so easy unless you already know the answer:

Hitty Pitty within the wall,

Hitty Pitty without the wall.

If you touch Hitty Pitty,

Hitty Pitty will bite you.

WHO or WHAT is Hitty Pitty?

⭐ **ANSWER:** Hitty Pitty is a stinging nettle!

WELCOME
TO THE WORLD OF
RIDDLES

Some of them, like Hitty Pitty, will **STING** you. Some of them will **SURPRISE** you. Some of them will make you **LAUGH.** I hope you will have fun with all of them.

TOP TIP: WHEN UNRAVELLING A RIDDLE, DON'T RUSH. Take your time. Think carefully about the question before you come up with your answer.

I am going to start with some **CLASSIC RIDDLES** – they are the oldest riddles in the book. And I am going to end with the 100 BEST (AND WORST) RIDDLES IN THE WORLD. In between you will find **WORD RIDDLES** and PICTURE RIDDLES, STORY RIDDLES and **RHYMING RIDDLES** – and **RIDICULOUS RIDDLES**, too. (They are my favourite.)

At the beginning of most chapters, I will give you a few riddles with their answers so that you can figure out how the riddles work. Then I will just give you the riddling questions – with the answers **HIDDEN** at the end of the chapter.

Don't **CHEAT** and sneak a peek until you have thought of an answer yourself.

Good luck!

Have fun.

**By the way, what goes up WHITE
and comes down YELLOW?**

 ANSWER: *An egg – if you throw it in the air
and don't catch it.*

For some reason (nobody knows why),
EGGS feature in lots of riddles.

I have a LITTLE house, which I live in all ALONE,

Without doors, without windows.

And if I want to go out I have

to break through the wall.

WHAT AM I?

ANSWER: *An egg, of course.*

Eggs even feature in riddles that are really just jokes. CHARLES DICKENS wrote a famous book called *Great Expectations*.

What book did CHARLES CHICKENS write?

Great Eggspectations.

ENOUGH!

Or, as they say in France, *'Un oeuf!'*

'UN OEUF' is French for **'AN EGG'**.
(That was also much more of a joke than a riddle. And a great example of a PUN!)

Which reminds me:

What do you find in the middle of PARIS?

You find it close to the middle of BERLIN, too.

It's there when you arrive in ROME,

but nowhere to be seen in LONDON.

WHAT IS IT?

 ANSWER: *The letter 'R'.*

Now that really is *UN OEUF*. On with the riddles!

CHAPTER 2
CLASSIC
RIDDLES

The **GREAT** Greek writer HOMER, who lived 3,000 years ago, had a lot of trouble with this riddle. It was put to him by some fishermen he met on the Greek island of Ios.

What we caught, we THREW AWAY;
What we didn't catch, we KEPT.

 The **ANSWER** is a lousy one because it's **LICE**!

If you have ever had lice in your hair, you'll know the riddle works: the lice you catch you **THROW AWAY**; the lice you can't catch you **KEEP**.

Not quite so long ago – in fact, only 1,400 years ago – a **MONK** called the VENERABLE BEDE, who lived in Northumbria in the north-east of England, conjured up some very **CRAFTY** riddles.

Tell me, what is it that fills the sky and the whole earth, tears up new shoots and shakes all foundations, but cannot be seen by eyes or touched by hands?

 **ANSWER:** *The wind.*

Here is another of Bede's **BEST**. Unravelling this riddle isn't easy.

I am sitting ABOVE a horse that was not born,

whose mother I HOLD in my hand.

WHAT AM I?

 ANSWER: *A horse drawn by a pen. Bede is sitting at his desk, looking down at a drawing of a horse. He is above the horse because he is looking down at it. And, because the horse is only a drawing, it was never born. It was created by a pen or a pencil – its mother – that Bede is holding in his hand.*

Another MONK who loved riddles was DR CLARETUS, who lived 600 years ago in Bohemia – now the Czech Republic. Dr Claretus produced **TERRIBLE TEASERS**, like this:

Like grass it is GREEN, but it is not grass,

Like blood it is RED, but it is not blood.

It is ROUND and SMOOTH like an egg.

WHAT IS IT?

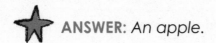 **ANSWER:** *An apple.*

This next one isn't **easy**, but it's very **clever**.

A vessel have I

That is round as a pear,

Moist in the middle,

Surrounded with hair;

And often it happens

That water flows there.

ANSWER: *An eye. An eye looks a bit like a pear on its side; an eye is wet and squidgy, so it's moist in the middle; and your eyelashes and eyebrows mean it's surrounded with hair. And, when you cry, 'water flows there'.*

Here is an **OLD RIDDLE** that comes from **Iceland**:

Four are hanging,

Four are walking,

Two point the way out,

Two ward the dogs off,

One ever dirty

Dangles behind it.

WHAT AM I?

⭐ **ANSWER:** *A cow – she has four teats on her udder, four legs to walk on, two horns on her head, two back legs, and one dirty tail.*

Two hundred and fifty years ago an Englishman called CHARLES JAMES FOX created this riddle, now regarded as a **CLASSIC**:

**I WENT to the Crimea;
I STOPPED there, and I never WENT there,
and I came back again.
WHAT AM I?**

ANSWER: *A watch. The watch travelled with Fox to the Crimea. The watch stopped going when Fox was out there, never worked while he was there, and Fox then brought the watch back home.*

The **BEST** riddles stand the test of time. See if you are foxed by these OLD FAVOURITES. They have been around for hundreds of years. When you get used to the **OLD-FASHIONED** way they are worded, you will find they are not as **TRICKY** as they first appear.

REMEMBER that **TOP TIP**
and **TAKE YOUR TIME.**

1. It has CITIES, but no **houses**;
It has FORESTS, but no **trees**;
It has RIVERS, but no **fish**.
WHAT IS IT?

2. As I was going over LONDON BRIDGE,
I saw something in the **hedge**.
It had **four fingers** and **one thumb**,
And was neither fish, flesh, fowl nor bone.
WHAT WAS IT?

3. LONG NECK and **no hands**,
HUNDRED LEGS and **can't stand**,
Runs through the house of a morning,
Stands behind the door when company comes.
WHAT IS IT?

4. What has EYES but never **sees**?

What has a TONGUE but never **talks**?

What has a SOUL that can't be **saved**?

5. I tremble at each **breath of air**,

And yet can HEAVIEST burdens bear.

WHAT AM I?

6. When it has a ROOT, it has no **leaves**;

When it PULLS up its root, the leaves APPEAR.

WHAT IS IT?

7. I SAT and I **ate**,

and FROM ME one **ate**,

And BELOW ME one **ate**,

and ABOVE ME one **ate**.

HOW COULD THIS BE?

8. As I was going to WORCESTER,

I met a man from **Gloucester**.

I asked him where he was going,

And he told me to **Gloucester**,

To buy something that had neither top nor bottom,

But which could hold flesh, blood and bones.

WHAT WAS IT?

9. It's **ten** men's STRENGTH,

and **ten** men's LENGTH,

And **ten** men cannot set it on end,

Yet **one** man can **carry** it.

WHAT IS IT?

10. There is a kind of TREE

that you can cut down **today**,

And **tomorrow** it will begin to SPROUT again.

WHAT IS IT?

11. The man who MADE it did not **want** it;

The man who BOUGHT it did not **use** it;

The man who USED it did not **know** it.

WHAT IS IT?

12. The AIR alone gives BIRTH to this;

It LIVES without a **body**;

It HEARS without **ears**;

It SPEAKS without a **mouth**.

WHAT IS IT?

13. A **messenger** who could not SPEAK, bearing a **letter** that was not WRITTEN, came to a **city** that had no FOUNDATIONS.

WHO was the **messenger**?

WHAT was the **letter**?

WHERE was the **city**?

(**HINT:** The answers are in a famous story from the Bible, as well as on page 36.)

14. What do you LOSE every time you **stand up**?

15. Can you make a FIRE with only one STICK?

16. It LIVES in **winter**,

DIES in **summer**,

And grows with its root upward.

WHAT IS IT?

17. If you FEED it, it will **live**;

If you GIVE IT WATER, it will **die**.

WHAT IS IT?

18. I've SEEN you where you NEVER were,

And where you ne'er will be;

And yet you in that very same place

May STILL be SEEN by me.

WHAT AM I?

19. What can go up the chimney DOWN,
But can't go down the chimney UP?

20. Two legs SAT upon three legs,
One leg KNOCKED two legs off three legs,
Two legs HIT four legs with three legs!
CAN YOU WORK OUT WHAT HAPPENED?

21. What has a **bed** but never SLEEPS
and has a **mouth** yet never EATS?

22. At night they come without being
fetched, and by day they are lost without being
stolen. **WHAT ARE THEY?**

23. As I went across the **bridge**, I met a man with a load of wood that was neither straight nor crooked. What kind of wood was it?

24. What is FILLED every **morning** and EMPTIED every **night**, except once a year when it is FILLED at **night** and EMPTIED in the **morning**?

ANSWERS

1. *A map.*

2. *A glove.*

3. *A broom.*

4. *A shoe.*

5. *Water.*

6. *A ship at anchor.*
(The leaves are the ship's sails.)

7. *A woman feeding her baby is sitting on a horse beneath a cherry tree. She eats, the baby eats, the horse grazes, and a bird in the tree eats.*

8. *A ring.*

9. *A rope.*

10. *Hair.*

11. *A coffin.*

12. *An echo.*

13. *The messenger was a dove; the*

'letter' was an olive leaf; and the 'city' was on Noah's ark.

14. Your lap.

15. Yes, if it's a matchstick.

16. An icicle.

17. Fire.

18. Your reflection in a mirror.

19. An umbrella.

20. Someone (with two legs), who was sitting on a three-legged stool milking a cow (with four legs), was kicked by the cow, so the person hit the cow with the stool.

21. A river.

22. Stars.

23. Sawdust.

24. A stocking.

CHAPTER 3

WHAT NEXT?

What is the name of the SCOTTISH inventor and pioneer of steam engines who had a unit of power named after him?

⭐ **ANSWER:** *Watt. Yes, Watt is <u>actually</u> the name of the Scottish inventor and pioneer of steam engines who had a unit of power named after him. He was **James Watt** (1736–1819), and he invented the **Watt steam engine** in 1776, developed the idea of 'horsepower' as a unit of measurement for power, and had the 'watt' – the international unit for measuring power – named after him.*

That was a **REAL-LIFE** question with a **pun** for an answer!

What next? A chapter of riddles that all include the same word. **WHAT?** Yes, that's the word –

1. I am TAKEN from a **mine**,
and shut up in a **wooden case**,
from which I am never RELEASED,
and yet I am used by almost everybody.
WHAT AM I?

2. TWENTY of me will FIT in a **box**,

but ONE of me will FILL a **barn**.

WHAT AM I?

3. You can take away my FIRST letter,

and my SECOND letter.

You can take away ALL my letters –

and yet I **remain** the SAME.

WHAT AM I?

4. WHAT runs round the GARDEN

without **moving**?

5. WHAT belongs to you,

but others **use** it MORE than you do?

6. WHAT is it that, the **more** you **take** away, the **larger** it becomes?

7. WHAT is **put** on a table, cut but never EATEN?

8. WHAT is always **coming** but never arrives?

9. WHAT invention allows you to SEE through **walls**?

10. WHAT happened when the man SAT on a **pin**?

11. WHAT was the HIGHEST mountain in the **world** before Mount Everest was discovered?

12. WHAT can PASS before the **sun** without casting a **shadow**?

13. WHAT has FOUR **legs** and ONE **back** but can't walk?

14. WHAT has only TWO **backbones** but a THOUSAND **ribs**?

15. WHAT has a **neck** but no **head**?

16. WHAT has a **face** but no **mouth**?

17. WHAT have **feet** and **legs** and nothing else?

18. WHAT has FOUR **legs**, ONE **head** and a **foot**?

19. WHAT can you keep after **giving** it to someone else?

20. WHAT question can **never** be answered 'Yes'?

21. WHAT is **big** at the BOTTOM, **little** at the TOP and has **ears**?

ANSWERS

1. A pencil lead.
(Lead is taken from a mine and used in a pencil!)

2. A candle.
(A lit candle will fill a barn with light.)

3. A postie.

4. A garden fence.

5. Your name.

6. A hole.

7. A pack of playing cards.

8. Tomorrow.

9. The window.

10. Nothing – it was a safety pin.
(Tee-hee!)

11. *Mount Everest.*
(It was still the highest mountain, even if it hadn't been discovered.)

12. *The wind.*

13. *A chair.*

14. *A railway track.*

15. *A bottle.*

16. *A clock.*

17. *Stockings.*

18. *A bed.*

19. *Your word.*

20. *'Are you asleep?'*

21. *A mountain.*
(It has mountain-eers!)

CHAPTER 4

FOOD

FOR

THOUGHT

Here are **nine TASTY RIDDLES** suitable for **vegetarians**. The answers are all **meat-free**.

WARNING: These **VEGGIE RIDDLES** are not all suitable for **vegans**. **Eggs** and **dairy** may be involved. (I did warn you that there are a lot of **EGGS** in the world of riddles, didn't I?)

EGGSACTLY!

1. You are looking at a green house.
Inside the green house there is a white house.
Inside the white house there is a red house.
Inside the red house there are a lot of
little black beetles.
WHAT ARE YOU LOOKING AT?

2. What goes over the fields all DAY
and sits in the fridge all NIGHT?

3. What vegetable do you **THROW** away the outside, **COOK** the inside, **EAT** the outside and throw away the inside?

4. It **STANDS** on its one leg, with its heart in its head.
WHAT IS IT?

5. Patch upon patch without any stitches –

Riddle me that, and I'll buy you

a pair of breeches.

WHAT IS IT?

6. What kind of ear cannot hear?

7. A family of farmers had EGGS
for **BREAKFAST** every morning.
They owned no chickens and didn't
get **EGGS** from anybody else.
WHERE DID THEY GET THE EGGS?

8. What **TWO** things
can't you have for breakfast?

9. If it takes three and a half minutes
to boil an **EGG**, how long does it
take to boil four **EGGS?**

ANSWERS

1. *A watermelon.*

2. *Milk.*

3. *Corn on the cob.*

4. *An artichoke.*

5. *A cabbage. (Cabbages are grown in cabbage patches.)*

6. *An ear of corn.*

7. *From their ducks.*

8. *Lunch and dinner.*

9. *Three and a half minutes – if they're all boiled at the same time!*

CHAPTER 5
MAKING A SPLASH!

There are no **EGGS** in this chapter, but there is an **EGG CUP** – and lots of water. Dive in and UNRAVEL these eleven **RIDDLES**, if you can. (By the way, what do you call a WATERING CAN with a leaky bottom? A **WATERING CAN'T**. OKAY, OKAY, I know that was more of a **SILLY JOKE** than a **REAL RIDDLE**, but I couldn't resist it!)

1. What is **round** as a DISHPAN, **deep** as a TUB and still the **oceans** couldn't fill it up?

2. FIVE girls stood under a SMALL **umbrella** but none of them got **wet**. HOW WAS THAT POSSIBLE?

3. What holds **water** yet is **FULL** of **holes**?

4. What is it that **NEVER freezes**?

5. Crooked as a **RAINBOW**,
Slick as a **PLATE**,
TEN THOUSAND horses
Can't pull it **straight**.
WHAT IS IT?

6. What has FOUR eyes but cannot see?

7. When will a net hold WATER?

8. What often falls but never gets hurt?

9. There were FIVE people going along a path when it began to rain. The FOUR who started running all got wet, but the ONE who remained still stayed dry. HOW COME?

10. A man went for a **walk**.

It started to **rain**.

The man didn't have a **hat**.

He wasn't CARRYING an **umbrella**.

He kept on WALKING.

His **clothes** got wet.

His **shoes** got wet.

But his **hair** didn't get wet.

HOW COME?

11. There is a **bathtub** filled with water
in front of you. You have a **spoon**,
an **egg cup**, a **mug** and a **bucket**.
WHAT IS THE QUICKEST WAY
TO EMPTY THE BATHTUB?

ANSWERS

1. *A sieve.*

2. *It wasn't raining.*

3. *A sponge.*

4. *Hot water.*

5. *A river.*

6. *The Mississippi River.*

7. *When the water is frozen into ice.*

8. *Rain.*

9. *They were in a funeral procession. The person in the coffin stayed dry, while the four people carrying the coffin got wet.*

10. *He was bald.*

11. *Pull out the bath plug!*

CHAPTER 6
FAMILY MATTERS

Remember that **TOP TIP:**

take your time and think carefully here.

With these **PUZZLING RIDDLES**, it's easy to

JUMP to the wrong conclusion . . .

1. There are TWO **Canadians** walking down the street. **ONE Canadian** is the father of the other Canadian's **son**. HOW COME?

2. A boy's **grandfather** is only FIVE years older than the boy's **father**. HOW COME?

3. Is it POSSIBLE for a man to **marry** his widow's **sister**?

4. Your uncle's **sister** is RELATED to you, but she's not your **aunt**. WHO IS SHE?

5. A man is looking at a **PHOTOGRAPH** of a member of his **family**. He says, 'Brothers and sisters have I none, but that man's **father** is my father's **son**.' **WHO IS IN THE PHOTOGRAPH?**

6. What's the **LEAST** number of chairs you would need round a table to sit **FOUR** fathers, **TWO** grandfathers and **FOUR sons**?

ANSWERS

1. *The two Canadians are a mother and father – they are both parents of the son.*

2. *The boy's grandfather is his mother's father, not his father's father.*

3. *No – if his wife is a widow, he's dead.*

4. *Your mother.*

5. *His son.*

6. *Four. The four fathers could be grandfathers and are definitely sons already.*

CHAPTER 7
WORDS, WORDS, WORDS - AND CROSSWORDS, TOO

Here is an **EASY RIDDLE**:

**What comes ONCE in a minute,
TWICE in a moment but not ONCE
in a thousand years?**

 ANSWER: *The letter 'M'.*

This **RIDDLE** isn't so easy:

**What FIVE-letter word leaves SIX
when you take TWO away?**

ANSWER: *Sixty. 'SIXTY' is a five-letter word
– take away the last two letters ('T' and 'Y') and
you are left with 'SIX'.*

When it comes to solving **RIDDLES** involving
WORDS and **LETTERS**, it can help to have some
PAPER and a PENCIL handy. You can jot down
ideas as you try to work out your answer.

It's time to dip your spoon into this **alphabet soup** of **RIDDLES** all about **words**, **letters** and the **English language**.

1. What EIGHT-letter word has ONE letter in it?

2. What TWO words have THOUSANDS of letters in them?

3. When is it correct to say 'I is'?

4. Where does Thursday come before Wednesday?

5. Luke had it FIRST.
Paul had it LAST.
Boys never have it.
Girls have it but ONCE.
WHAT IS IT?

6. There is a word in the **English** language, the first **TWO** letters of which signify a **male**, the first **THREE** a **female**, the first **FOUR** a great man and the **WHOLE** a great woman.

WHAT IS THE WORD?

7. What word of **THREE** syllables contains **TWENTY-SIX letters?**

8. What part of **London** is in **France?**

The first **SIX** lines in this **RHYMING RIDDLE** will lead you to one or more different letters of the ALPHABET. Look at the letters carefully and then choose just **SIX** of them – **ONE** from each line – to form the six-letter word that is the FINAL answer.

9. My FIRST is in **south** but not in **north**,
My SECOND is in **picture** but not in **film**,
My THIRD is in **fourth** and also in **worth**,
My FOURTH is in **book** and also in **cook**,
My FIFTH is in **toe** but not in **sew**,
My SIXTH is in **life** but not in **death**.
My WHOLE is a **place** you all must go!

The first **FIVE** lines in this **RHYMING RIDDLE** will lead you to one or more different letters of the ALPHABET. Look at the letters carefully and then choose **FIVE** of them – **ONE** from each line - to form the **FIVE-LETTER** word that is the FINAL answer.

10. My **FIRST** is in **apple** and also in **pear**,
My **SECOND** is in **desperate** and also in **dare**,
My **THIRD** is in **sparrow** and also in **lark**,
My **FOURTH** is in **cashier** and also in **clerk**,
My **FIFTH** is in **seven** and also in **ten**,
My **WHOLE** is a blessing indeed unto **men**.

What's a cross word? **ANGRY** is a cross word.
FURIOUS is an even crosser word.

What's a **CROSSWORD?**

That's a different question!

A **CROSSWORD** is a WORD PUZZLE that
usually takes the form of a square grid of WHITE
and BLACK squares. The aim of the **PUZZLE** is
to SOLVE clues to find the words that fit into
the WHITE squares.

A **HUNDRED** years ago, when the
CROSSWORD first became POPULAR,
the clues were SIMPLE ones.

CLUE: The capital of France.

 ANSWER: *PARIS.*

Lots of **CROSSWORDS** still have SIMPLE clues, but some have **'CRYPTIC CLUES'**, which are really **RIDDLES**.

CLUE: They came in two by two – in the capital of France.

 ANSWER: *PAIRS.*

PAIRS come in twos, don't they? And you will find the letters **'P'**, **'A'**, **'I'**, **'R'** and **'S'** in the capital of France: **PARIS**.

CLEVER STUFF, EH?

The English word **'CRYPTIC'** comes from the ancient GREEK word **'KRYPTEIN'**, which means **'TO HIDE'** and, in CRYPTIC crossword puzzle clues, the answer is **HIDING** in the clue. Often, the answer is hiding INSIDE one or two words in the clue and to find the answer you have to **REARRANGE** the letters in THOSE words to come up with a **DIFFERENT** word that uses the SAME letters.

FOR EXAMPLE, if the clue is **'THEY SEE'**, the answer is **'THE EYES'**.

Words that can be REARRANGED into other words are called **ANAGRAMS**.

SWORD
is an anagram of
WORDS.

Take EACH of these TEN words and phrases and **TURN THEM INTO** a different word or phrase to finish the sentence. The first few are *easy*. The last few are *FIENDISH*.

TIP: Write down the letters in the **FIRST** word in a CIRCLE on a piece of paper and begin to rearrange them in your head. I've done the first one for you. Makes it a bit easier, doesn't it?

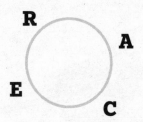

11. Don't **RACE**, take _ _ _ _.

12. This **PEACH** is not expensive; it's _ _ _ _ _.

13. LISTEN, it's time to be _ _ _ _ _ _.

14. You're not ILL-FED when you're well _ _ _ _ _ _.

15. On **MONDAY** I'm full of energy –
I'm a real _ _ _ _ _ _.

16. THE DETECTIVES _ _ _ _ _ _ / _ _ _ _ _ _ _.

17. An ELEGANT MAN is _ / _ _ _ _ _ _ _ _ _ _ _

18. 'A STEW, SIR?' asked the _ _ _ _ _ _ _ _.

19. I'M A DOT IN PLACE:
I'm _ / _ _ _ _ _ _ _ / _ _ _ _ _.

20. Looking up into the sky, **ASTRONOMERS** are
_ _ _ _ _ / _ _ _ _ _ _ _.

To **END** the CHAPTER, here is one more
CRYPTIC challenge. It's a **TOUGH ONE**.

21. You are looking for an everyday five-
letter word, and this is your clue:

H I J K L M N O.

WRITING DOWN the letters in a
CIRCLE won't really help you this time,
but **THINKING** about WHICH letters
of the alphabet they are might. The
letters run from **H** to **O**, don't they?

ANSWERS

1. *Envelope.*

2. *Post office.*

3. *When you say, 'I is the letter after H.'*

4. *In a dictionary.*

5. *The letter 'L'.*

6. *Heroine (he, her, hero, heroine).*

7. *Alphabet.*

8. *The letter 'N'.*

9. *School.*

10. *Peace.*

11. *CARE*

12. *CHEAP*

13. *SILENT*

14. *FILLED*

15. *DYNAMO*

16. *DETECT THIEVES*

17. *A GENTLEMAN*

18. *WAITRESS*

19. *A DECIMAL POINT*

20. *MOON STARERS*

21. *Water. (The letters H I J K L M N O take you from 'H' to 'O': the chemical symbol for water is H_2O.)*

CHAPTER 8

SURPRISE YOUR EYES

You **CAN'T BELIEVE** everything you SEE,

as you will **DISCOVER** with these

surprising picture riddles.

1. Is the hat taller or wider?

2. Which line is longer,

the top one or the bottom one?

3. How many of these lines are curved?

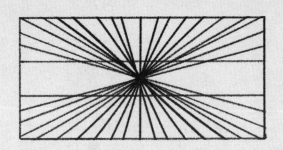

4. Which of the two shaded circles is bigger –
the one on the left or the one on the right?

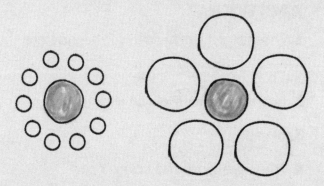

5. Is this a rabbit
or a duck?

6. Is the shaded side of the box
inside or outside?

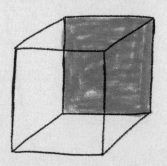

ANSWERS

1. *The height and width of the hat are exactly the same.*

2. *Both lines are the same length.*

3. *None.*

4. *They are both the same size.*

5. *It can be either – or both!*

6. *It can be inside or outside, depending on how it strikes you.*

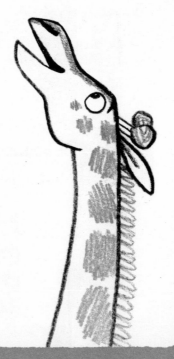

CHAPTER 9

RIDDLE
MYSTERIES

There are **FIVE** boys locked in a room. ADAM is reading a book. BEN **is making a sandwich.** CHARLIE **is playing chess.** DANIEL is watching **TV. What is the FIFTH boy doing?**

REMEMBER the **TOP TIP:**

take your time, think it through . . .

Have you WORKED OUT what the **FIFTH** boy is doing? He is **PLAYING CHESS** with Charlie, of course. You can read a BOOK, make a SANDWICH and watch TV on your own, but you **CAN'T** play chess alone.

There are TWO GIRLS: one is facing NORTH, the other is facing SOUTH, yet they can see each other without using mirrors.

HOW COME?

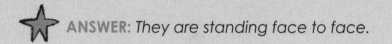

WELCOME

to the world of **RIDDLE MYSTERIES**, where you have to PICTURE the **SCENE** and think very carefully to be able to solve the **MYSTERY** in question.

1

THE CASE OF TOM, DICK, HARRY AND LARRY

TOM, **DICK**, HARRY and **LARRY** all lived together in the same house. One night **TOM** and **DICK** went out for a meal. When they got back at about **MIDNIGHT**, they were horrified to find **LARRY** lying dead in a pool of water on the floor. They knew that HARRY was the murderer, but they didn't tell the police. **HOW COME?**

2

THE CASE OF
THE ONE-WAY STREET

A POLICE OFFICER saw a **LORRY DRIVER**
going the **WRONG WAY** down a one-way street,
but didn't stop him. **WHY NOT?**

3

THE CASE OF
THE WANDERING BEAR

Once upon a time there was a BEAR that
decided to go for a WALK. The bear walked
1 mile SOUTH. The bear then turned and walked
1 mile EAST. The bear then turned again and
walked 1 mile NORTH. The bear ended up
EXACTLY where it had begun.
WHAT COLOUR WAS THE BEAR?

4

THE CASE OF
THE TWO JOLLY BUTCHERS

There are two **JOLLY BUTCHERS** standing

behind a COUNTER in a **SHOP**.

One butcher is SHORT and the other butcher

is TALL. The tall butcher is the FATHER of the

short butcher, but the short butcher is NOT

the son of the tall butcher.

HOW ARE THEY RELATED?

5

THE CASE OF THE SAD MAN

With a heavy heart, a **SAD** man pushed his

CAR up to a **HOTEL**. He was sad because he

knew he had lost all his MONEY.

WHAT WAS GOING ON?

6

THE CASE OF
THE RISING TIDE

You are on board your private YACHT, moored

off the coast of an island in the South Pacific.

Hanging over the side of the yacht is a LADDER

with twelve rungs.

The distance between each RUNG is

50 centimetres and the lowest rung is just

touching the SURFACE of the water.

The TIDE is coming in and the water is rising at a

rate of 10 centimetres an hour. HOW SOON will

the surface of the water cover the

SIXTH RUNG from the top of the ladder?

7

THE CASE OF
THE WEATHER FORECASTER

The **WEATHER FORECASTER** woke up in the

middle of the night and, much to his surprise,

found that it was **POURING** with rain.

He hadn't expected it to rain that night

because it was SUMMERTIME.

However, now he had seen the rain,

he predicted that in **72 HOURS' TIME** there

would still be no sign of SUNNY weather.

HOW COULD HE BE SO SURE?

THE CASE OF
THE SILENT PARROT

Polly Kettle decided to buy herself a

TALKING PARROT as a pet. She went to the

pet shop, where the assistant showed her a
BEAUTIFUL bird and told her, 'I guarantee that
this parrot will repeat EVERY word
it hears.' Polly bought the parrot
and took it home, where she quickly
discovered that the PARROT would not
and COULD NOT speak a single word.
Strangely the pet-shop assistant had
only told Polly the TRUTH.
CAN YOU EXPLAIN THE MYSTERY?

THE CASE OF THE BOY IN THE BLOCK OF FLATS

TOM BROWN is a young schoolboy who lives
in the **TALLEST** block of flats in Manchester.
Every day he goes to school and gets
the LIFT from his flat on the
THIRTY-NINTH floor to the ground.

Every afternoon, when he comes home
from school, he takes the lift to the
TWENTY-NINTH floor and WALKS up
the remaining flights of stairs.
The lift works perfectly well, and
Tom Brown does not need to EXERCISE,
so **WHY DOES HE DO IT?**

10

THE CASE OF
HANK AND THE TWO BARBERS

In the days of the old Wild West, a COWBOY
called Hank rolled into a ramshackle town in
the heart of Texas. Hank had been out on the
trail for more than a month and he needed
a SHAVE and a **HAIRCUT.** He quickly
discovered that the town only had two
BARBERS, each one with his own shop.
Hank looked inside the FIRST shop, where he

saw the barber looking very smart, cleanly SHAVEN and with his hair well groomed and neatly cut. Hank then looked into the SECOND barber's shop. The place was in a DREADFUL mess and the barber himself was unshaven and had long, shaggy hair. Hank gave the matter a little thought and then decided to use the SECOND barber for his shave and haircut.

WHY?

11

THE CASE OF THE MARTIAN AND THE VENUSIAN

You are lost in space. You have landed on an ALIEN planet. It could be VENUS or it could be MARS. All you know about Martians and Venusians is that Martians always tell the truth and Venusians always tell lies. You need to know where you are, so you stop an alien passer-by. You know the alien is either a MARTIAN or a VENUSIAN, but you don't know which. You are allowed to ask the alien just ONE SHORT QUESTION of not more than **FOUR** words to find out where you are.

WHAT IS THE QUESTION?

12
THE CASE OF THE THREE DOORS

There are **THREE DOORS** in front of you. You have to go through one of them.

Behind the **FIRST** door, a fire is raging.

Behind the SECOND door,

a masked gunman is lurking.

Behind the **THIRD** door is a lion

that hasn't eaten for three years.

**WHICH IS THE SAFEST DOOR
TO GO THROUGH?**

ANSWERS

1. *Larry was a goldfish and Harry was a cat.*

2. *The lorry driver was walking.*

3. *White. It was a polar bear. Only at the North Pole can a bear walk south for a mile, then east for a mile, then north for a mile and end up in the same place. Polar bears live in the Arctic, so the only bears you'll find at the North Pole are polar bears. (Down south in Antarctica you'll find penguins, seals, whales and all kinds of seabirds, but **never** polar bears.)*

4. *The short butcher is the **daughter** of the tall butcher.*

5. *The man was playing a game of Monopoly. His playing piece was a car, and he landed on a property with a hotel on it. This meant that, according to the rules of Monopoly, he had to pay the owner of the hotel.*

6. *It won't. The water will never cover the rung because, as the water rises, so does the yacht, and so does the ladder!*

7. In 72 hours' time it would be night-time again, so there certainly would not be any sunshine.

8. The parrot was deaf.

9. Tom Brown is a young schoolboy – he isn't tall enough to reach higher than the button for the twenty-ninth floor!

10. As there were only two barbers in the town, each must have cut the other's hair. Hank chose the barber who had given his rival the cleaner shave and better haircut.

11. 'Do you live here?' If you are on Mars, the answer will be 'Yes' because Martians always tell the truth and Venusians always lie. If you are on Venus, the answer will be 'No'.

12. The third door. A lion can only survive a week or two without food, so if it's three years since the lion last ate, the lion will be dead.

CHAPTER 10
RIDICULOUS
RIDDLES

SOME of these RIDDLES aren't as **silly** as they look. But SOME are **very** silly INDEED.

Number **twenty-two** is my FAVOURITE, and by far the SILLIEST.

1. How MANY **sweets** can you put into an **empty** bag?

2. How can you **leave** a room with TWO legs and COME BACK with **six** legs?

3. What stays **hot** in the REFRIGERATOR?

4. What **letters** are INVISIBLE, but NEVER out of **sight**?

5. If your **watch** is broken, WHY can't you go **fishing**?

6. WHY do you GO to **bed**?

7. What do most **gardeners** not LIKE to GROW?

8. If a **band** plays in a THUNDERSTORM, who is MOST LIKELY to get hit by **lightning**?

9. What kind of **band** DOESN'T make MUSIC?

10. How could you **fall off** a twenty-foot LADDER and not get HURT?

11. If you were to throw a **white** stone into the RED SEA, what would it BECOME?

12. What's the **difference** between HERE and THERE?

13. WHICH Member of Parliament wears the **largest hat**?

14. WHERE do all PEOPLE look EXACTLY the **same**?

15. Captain Cook made **three** voyages round the WORLD and was KILLED on ONE of them. **Which one**?

16. WHY did the little **girl** put her **HEAD** on the PIANO?

17. WHAT kind of person **always** tries to make you SMILE?

18. WHERE and WHEN can you **never** tell the **truth**?

19. Why did it take **three** Boy Scouts to help the OLD LADY across the **STREET**?

20. What ANIMAL is grey, has FOUR LEGS and a **trunk**?

21. I have a LOCKED safe that contains **two vases**. All that is known about the vases is that ONE is GOLD and ONE is **silver**. Is there ANY way I can find out their **colours** WITHOUT taking them **out** of the SAFE?

22. If frozen **water** is ICED water, what is frozen **ink**?

ANSWERS

1. *Only one. After that the bag isn't empty any more.*

2. *When you come back, carry a chair with you.*

3. *Mustard.*

4. *The letters 'I' and 'S'. (These letters are in 'visible', and in 'sight'. Get it?)*

5. *Because you haven't the time.*

6. *Because the bed won't come to you.*

7. *Old.*

8. *The conductor.*

9. *A rubber band.*

10. *Fall off the bottom rung.*

11. *Wet.*

12. *The letter 'T'.*

13. *The one with the largest head.*

14. *In the dark.*

15. *The last one.*

16. *She wanted to play by ear.*

17. *A photographer.*

18. *When you're lying in bed.*

19. *Because she didn't want to go.*

20. *A mouse moving house! (Well, the chapter is called 'Ridiculous Riddles'.)*

21. *Yes. One is gold and the other is silver.*

22. *Iced ink. (You stink, do you? I told you this was my favourite!)*

CHAPTER 11
RHYMING RIDDLES

*From the **RIDICULOUS** to the SUBLIME –*
*Or at least to RIDDLES that **RHYME!***

In **DAYS GONE BY**, many of
the BEST riddles were written in **rhyme**.
It made them **EASIER** to REMEMBER,
even if it **didn't** make them easier to **SOLVE!**

About a HUNDRED and **FIFTY** years ago,
the poet **Christina Rossetti** wrote this
RHYMING RIDDLE:

There is one that has a **HEAD** without an EYE,
And there's one that has an EYE without a **HEAD**.
You may find the **answer** if you TRY,
And, when all is **SAID**,
Half the ANSWER hangs upon a **thread**.

Do you know what the answer is?

It is a *pin* and a *needle*. Picture a pin and
picture a needle, then READ the riddle again –
you will see it **makes sense**.

The **PIN** is the *'one that has a head without an
eye'*. The NEEDLE is the *'one that has an eye
without a head'*.

Here are more **RHYMING RIDDLES** for you to unravel.

Remember that **TOP TIP** and TAKE YOUR TIME to think it through. And TRY TO PICTURE what the rhyming riddlers are writing about.

WARNING:
EGGS AHEAD!
(In the world of riddles, you're never far from an egg.)

1. In marble halls as white as **milk**,

Lined with a **skin** as soft as silk,

Within a FOUNTAIN crystal **clear**,

A golden **apple** doth appear.

No **doors** are there to this stronghold,

Yet thieves break in and steal the gold.

WHAT IS IT?

2. In **spring** I look gay,

Decked in comely array;

In **summer** more clothing I wear;

When colder it grows,

I fling off my **clothes**,

And in **winter** quite NAKED appear.

WHAT AM I?

Lewis Carroll, who wrote *Alice's Adventures in Wonderland*, loved rhyming riddles. Here's one he invented in 1870:

3. Three **sisters** at breakfast
were feeding the CAT.
The first gave it **sole** –
Puss was grateful for that.
The next gave it **salmon** –
which Puss thought a treat.
The third gave it **herring** –
which Puss WOULDN'T eat.
CAN YOU EXPLAIN the cat's behaviour?

J. R. R. TOLKIEN, who wrote *The Hobbit* and *The Lord of the Rings*, is another famous English writer who loved **RHYMING RIDDLES**.

Here are three of his favourites, which he actually used in *The Hobbit*:

4. What has **roots** as nobody sees,
Is taller than the **trees**,
Up, up it goes,
And yet **NEVER** grows?

5. It cannot be **seen**, cannot be felt,
Cannot be heard, cannot be **smelt**.
It lies behind STARS and under hills,
And empty **holes** it fills.
It comes **FIRST** and follows AFTER.
Ends life, **kills** laughter.
WHAT IS IT?

6. A **box** without hinges, key or lid.

Yet golden **treasure** inside is hid.

WHAT IS IT?

Old riddles now, and all in RHYME,

Crack each one and take your time;

Feast yourself, have a guzzle

On TWELVE sweet nuts, each one a **puzzle**.

7. Riddle me, riddle me, riddle me ree,

I saw a **nutcracker** up in a tree.

WHAT WAS IT?

8. LONG legs, CROOKED toes,

GLASSY eyes, SNOTTY nose.

WHAT IS IT?

9. Runs **smoother** than any rhyme,

Loves to FALL but cannot **climb**.

WHAT IS IT?

10. Goes to the **door** and doesn't KNOCK,

Goes to the **window** and doesn't RAP,

Goes to the **fire** and doesn't WARM,

Goes **upstairs** and does no HARM.

WHAT IS IT?

11. Riddle me, riddle me, what is **that**

OVER the head and **UNDER** the hat?

12. What's in the **church**,

but not the STEEPLE,

The **parson** has it, but not the **PEOPLE?**

13. Thirty white **horses** upon a red HILL,

Now they CHAMP, now they CLAMP,

And now they stand still.

WHAT ARE THEY?

14. As round as an **apple**,

As deep as a PAIL;

It **NEVER** cries out,

Till it's caught by the **tail**.

WHAT IS IT?

15. Formed long ago, yet made **today**,

EMPLOYED while others sleep;

What few would like to **give away**,

Nor many wish to KEEP.

WHAT IS IT?

16. What force of **strength**

cannot get through,

I, with GENTLE touch, can do;

And many in the street would **STAND**,

Were I not, as a friend, AT HAND.

WHAT AM I?

17. I washed my hands with **water**,

Which was **NEITHER** rain nor run,

I dried them on a **towel**,

Which was NEITHER woven nor spun.

HOW did I wash my hands?

HOW did I dry them?

18. Without a **bridle**,

Or a SADDLE,

Across a thing

I ride a-straddle,

And those I **ride**,

By help of me,

Though almost **blind**,

Are made to SEE.

WHAT AM I?

ANSWERS

1. *An egg.*

2. *A tree.*

3. *Lewis Carroll even put the answer into rhyme:*

That salmon and sole Puss should think very grand

Is no such remarkable thing.

For more of these dainties Puss took up her stand;

But when the third sister stretched out her fair hand

*Pray why should Puss swallow **her ring**?*

(Add a space, and 'herring' the fish becomes 'her ring'. Neat, eh?)

4. *A mountain.*

5. *Darkness.*

6. *Another egg – of course!*

7. *A squirrel.*

8. *A frog.*

9. *Rain.*

10. *Sunshine.*

11. *Hair.*

12. *The letter 'R'.*

13. *Teeth.*

14. *A bell.*

15. *A bed.*

16. *A key.*

17. *I washed my hands in dew and dried them in sunshine.*

18. *A pair of spectacles.*

CHAPTER 12

RIDDLES

WITH A

DIFFERENCE

Here's a **different** kind of riddle:

What is the difference between
a GREEDY PERSON and
an ELECTRIC TOASTER?

Shall I tell you?

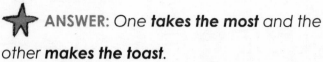 ANSWER: *One **takes the most** and the other **makes the toast**.*

Here's another one:

What is the difference between
a boy GOING upstairs and
a boy LOOKING upstairs?

Can you work it out?

ANSWER: *One is **stepping up the stairs**, while the other is **staring up the steps**.*

Here's a **MUCH MORE difficult** one:

What is the **difference** between
a **PUSSYCAT** and an ENGLISH SENTENCE?

⭐ ANSWER: *One has **claws** at the end of its
paws, the other has a **pause** at the end of its
clause.*

Now you've got the idea, have a go at these:

1. What is the **difference** between a
DOORMAT and a bottle of MEDICINE?

2. What is the **difference** between a
JEWELLER and a JAILER?

3. What is the **difference** between
a **HUNGRY** man and
a GREEDY man?

4. What is the **difference** between
a crazy **RABBIT** and
a counterfeit COIN?

5. What is the **difference** between
NOAH'S ARK and JOAN OF ARC?

6. What is the **difference** between
100 and 1,000?

7. What is the **difference** between
a **DOG** and a FLEA?

This next one is a **riddle** and a JOKE all mixed up. Try it on a friend.

You start by asking the **question**, then your **FRIEND** responds:

YOU: **What is the difference between a THUNDERSTORM,** a LION WITH TOOTHACHE **and a pot of glue?**

YOUR FRIEND: *I don't know.*

YOU: **The THUNDERSTORM pours with rain and the** LION WITH TOOTHACHE **roars with pain.**

YOUR FRIEND: *What about the little pot of glue?*

YOU: **That's where you get stuck.**

ANSWERS

1. *One is taken up and shaken, the other is shaken up and taken.*

2. *One sells watches, the other watches cells.*

3. *One longs to eat, the other eats too long.*

4. *One is a mad bunny, the other is bad money.*

5. *One was made of wood, the other was Maid of Orleans.*

6. *Nothing – well, 0 is nothing!*

7. *A dog can have fleas, but a flea can't have dogs.*

CHAPTER 13
ANIMAL CRACKERS

TWO COWS were standing in the middle of a field chatting about the weather. A DOG ran over the field towards them, looked up and asked, '*Do you think it looks like rain?*' One of the cows turned to the other cow, wide-eyed with amazement.

'*Imagine that,*' she said, '**a talking dog!**'

I **love** silly stories about **animals**.

This next one is probably my **FAVOURITE**:

Three **polar bears** woke up from their long winter's sleep on an ICEBERG near the North Pole.

Mother Bear got to her feet and stretched and said, '*I have a tale to tell*.'

Then **Father Bear** got to his feet and stretched and said, '*I have a tale to tell, too*.'

But **Baby Bear** just sat on the iceberg shivering, '*My tale is told*,' he said.

Here are some **RIDDLES** about **animals**.

Some of them are quite **SILLY**, too.

1. If a **daddy bull** eats THREE bales of hay
and a **baby bull** eats ONE bale,
how much hay will a **mummy bull** eat?

2. What kind of **bird** is always around
when there's something
to **EAT** or DRINK?

3. What has a **head** like a cat,
paws like a cat,
a **tail** like a cat,
even **claws** and **whiskers** like a cat,
but is **NOT** a cat?

4. What has **six legs**
but only walks with FOUR?

5. What has FOUR legs like an **elephant**,
a TRUNK like an **elephant**
and LOOKS just like an **elephant**,
but is NOT an elephant?

6. How did a dog tied to a **12-foot rope**, manage to walk **30 FEET**?

7. What goes to **sleep** with its **SHOES** on?

8. On the way to a waterhole, a **ZEBRA** met six **giraffes**. Each giraffe had three MONKEYS hanging from its neck. Each **monkey** had two BIRDS on its tail. How many **animals** were going to the WATERHOLE?

9. Why are **playing cards** like **WOLVES**?

10. I'm **out and about** all day, and yet I ALWAYS stay at home. **WHAT AM I?**

ANSWERS

1. *None. There is no such thing as a mummy bull.*

2. *A swallow.*

3. *A kitten.*

4. *A horse with a rider.*

5. *A picture of an elephant.*

6. *The rope wasn't tied to anything.*

7. *A horse.*

8. *One – only the zebra. The others were going away from the waterhole.*

9. *Because they come in packs.*

10. *A snail.*

CHAPTER 14
REBUS RIDDLES

What's a **REBUS**?

A **REBUS** is a RIDDLE in which words
and phrases are represented by
letters and numbers, like this:

T 4.00 PM

What does that mean? Not a lot until you stop
to think about it. It's the letter **'T'** followed by a
TIME of day. That's it!

ANSWER: *Teatime.*

How about this:

MAAWNAGYER

It's tricky. Written like this it should be a bit easier:

M a A w N a G y E R

I'll give you a **clue**. You are looking for the first four words of a famous **CHRISTMAS CAROL**. Now you see it, don't you? The Christmas carol, written in the 1890s, is called **'Away in a Manger'** and in the rebus the word **'away'** has been dropped in between letters in the word **'manger'**.

ANSWER: *AWAY in a MANGER.*

This next one is a bit different.

What have we here?

P O T O O O O O O O O

Any idea? Set out like this, you may find it easier:

P O T   O O O O O O O O

What is it? 'Pot' and then eight 'O's . . .

 ANSWER: *Potatoes.*

Now you've got the **idea**, have a go at **THESE**.

You should get the first one in a **flash**.

(And, yes, that *is* a clue. I am going

to give you clues here, because

some of these are **tough**.)

1. B O L T
T H

If you're feeling peckish, you will need this.

2.
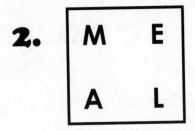
M   E
A   L

You could cover your duvet with this.

3. **B** **E** **D**

You are looking for just **one** word here –
WHICHEVER way you look at it . . .

4. **D N U O R**

You are looking for **four** words here . . .

5.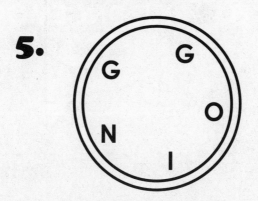

This will help you destroy **bacteria**.

6. FECDISTANT

This **doesn't** happen often.

7. THEFLASHPAN

This happens even **less** often!

8. BLUEONCEMOON

You could begin a **fairytale** with the FOUR
words you are looking for here.

9. ONCE
NOON

Keep **smiling**.

10. JOKE
U

Five letters leading you to five words that mean
something **identical** . . .

11. PPPOD

This is a phrase used to describe things
that are very **similar** . . .

12. ONEANOTHER
ONEANOTHER
ONEANOTHER
ONEANOTHER
ONEANOTHER
ONEANOTHER

This one is **painful**:

13. EHCA

You've been **caught**.

14. S N O O Z E
U R

What's this? A **container** of a kind . . .

15. C A T N

What have we here?
A **NUMBER**, and a lot of **water** . . .

16. C C C C C C

You might say this next one when you come home **HUNGRY**, open the FRIDGE and find **nothing** inside . . .

17. OICURMT

Happy?

18. HEAD
HEEL
HEEL

Embarrassed?

19. THEFREDACE

First past the post?

20. WINEEEEEE

21. STAND
TRY 2

Gone but not forgotten!

22. ABCDE
FGHIJ
KLMNO
PQRST
VWXYZ
already

ANSWERS

1. *Thunderbolt.*
2. *Square meal.*
3. *Bedspread.*
4. *Roundabout.*
5. *Going round in circles.*
6. *Disinfectant.*
7. *Flash in the pan.*
8. *Once in a blue moon.*
9. *Once upon a time*
10. *The joke's on you.*
11. *Two peas in a pod.*
12. *Six of one and half a dozen of another.*
13. *Backache.*
14. *You are under arrest.*
15. *Tin can.*
16. *The seven seas.*
17. *Oh, I see you are empty.*
18. *Head over heels.*
19. *Red in the face.*
20. *Win with ease.*
21. *Try to understand.*
22. *Missing you already.*

CHAPTER 15

YOUR
NUMBER'S
UP

How can you halve **eight** and end up with nothing?

Separate the top and bottom halves of the number eight and what are you left with? Two zeros!

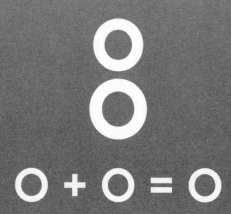

Now we've got eight out of the way, we are left with just seven **number** riddles – but what a **MAGNIFICENT** seven!

1. I am an **odd** number.

Take away a letter and I become even.

WHAT NUMBER am I?

2. If two's **company**,

and three's a crowd,

what are FOUR and **FIVE**?

3. What **three** numbers,

none of which is zero,

give the **SAME RESULT** whether

they're ADDED or multiplied?

4. What is BIGGER
when it's **upside down**?

5. Why is the number **ten**
like the number **ELEVEN**?

6. If you dug a HOLE
120 centimetres **wide**,
100 centimetres **long** and
75 centimetres **deep**,
HOW MUCH EARTH would be in it?

7. What **yard** has four **FEET** in it?

ANSWERS

1. *Seven.*

2. *Nine. (Four and five add up to nine!)*

3. *One, two and three.*
(1 + 2 + 3 = 6 and 1 x 2 x 3 = 6.)

4. *The number 6 – upside down it becomes the number 9.*

5. *Because twice ten is twenty, and twice eleven is twenty-two. (Get it?!* **Twenty too!***)*

6. *None, of course!*

7. *A farmyard, if it has a horse or a sheep or a dog in it.*

CHAPTER 16

ON THE MOVE

1. What goes **out** but **NEVER** comes back?

2. What goes **uphill** and **downhill** but **NEVER** moves?

3. What has a **thousand legs** and **CAN'T** walk?

4. What goes from **house** to **house** but **NEVER** goes inside?

5. What goes **round** and **round** the WOOD but never gets **INTO** the wood?

6. What **WALKS** all day on its **head**?

7. What goes **up** and
NEVER comes **down**?

8. What is it that an **aeroplane**
always travels with,
CANNOT travel without,
but is of **no use** to the aeroplane?

9. The **more** you take,
the **more** you leave behind.
WHAT ARE THEY?

10. What goes
UP and DOWN stairs
without moving?

11. What has four **wings**
and can't fly, and
no **LEGS** but
can keep **moving?**

12. What has no **legs**
and no **feet**
but runs along
most of the **STREETS** in town?

ANSWERS

1. *Your breath.*

2. *A road.*

3. *Five hundred pairs of trousers.*

4. *A path.*

5. *The bark of a tree.*

6. *A nail in a horseshoe.*

7. *Smoke.*

8. *Noise.*

9. *Footsteps.*

10. *Carpet.*

11. *A windmill.*

12. *The kerb.*

CHAPTER 17

DO-IT-YOURSELF

Are you any good at **DIY**?

Can you model with

plasticine or **clay**?

Could you, for example,
make a model of **this**?

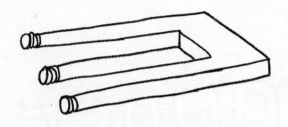

It's a **trick question**, because,
even if you **THINK** you could,
you COULDN'T.

There are some things that
can be **DRAWN**, but can't be **made**.

Look at this **box**:

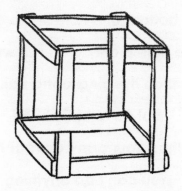

Believe it or not, even the cleverest

CARPENTER in the world couldn't make it.

It's a box you can design, but can't construct.

Odd, isn't it?

From two **impossible** DIY challenges,

let's turn to some others

that are POSSIBLE –

just.

1. You have a **ping-pong ball**

at the bottom of a hole in the ground.

The hole is only a LITTLE wider

than the ping-pong ball,

but it's a lot **DEEPER**

than your arm can reach.

You can't do anything

to extend your **arm**,

so what can you do to

get the ball **out** of the hole?

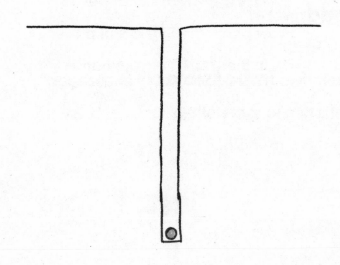

2. Take a ten-pound note

and a 10p piece.

Now try to BALANCE the 10p

on the **edge** of the ten-pound note.

CAN IT BE DONE?

3. TEAR UP a piece of paper

so that you have

five small bits of paper.

Now place the five bits of paper

in the **palm** of your hand

and BLOW them off

one by one.

It can be done.

Can **YOU** do it?

4. For this **DIY** riddle you'll need a large sheet of NEWSPAPER and a **FRIEND**.

How can TWO PEOPLE **stand** on the *same* sheet of newspaper, face to face, so that they can't SEE or **TOUCH** each other?
Their hands aren't tied, their **eyes** aren't closed or covered, and the sheet of newspaper must not be **torn**. It can be done.
CAN YOU DO IT?

5. In 1492 Christopher Columbus
didn't just sail the **ocean blue**,
he also invented a most UNUSUAL riddle.
This one:

Can you take a hard-boiled **egg**
and make it **STAND** on its end
WITHOUT wobbling?

ANSWERS

1. Pour water into the hole so that the ping-pong ball floats up to the surface.

2. Yes, but before you can balance the coin on the edge of the ten-pound note you have to fold the note into a shape like this:

3. Use your fingers to hold four of the pieces of paper while you blow one off. Then hold three and blow another one off. Then hold two, and so on.

4. To unravel the riddle you need a doorway. Place the sheet of newspaper on the floor so that one half of the sheet is one side of the door and the other half of the sheet is on the other side of the door. Then close the door!

5. This is how Christopher Columbus did it: He tapped one end of the egg against the table, crushing the tip of the shell so that the egg would stand up on its own. We riddlers can't get away from those eggs, can we?

CHAPTER 18
PICTURE
RIDDLES

What's THIS?

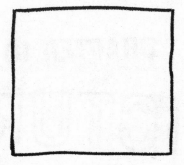

 ANSWER: A picture of two **polar bears** playing in a **snowstorm**, of course!

What's THIS?

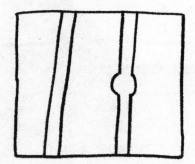

 ANSWER: A picture of a **stork** with a wooden leg!

Now you've got the idea, have a go at
unravelling these **PICTURE** riddles.

1. What's THIS?

2. What's THIS?

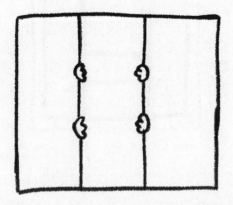

3. What's THIS?

4. What's THIS?

5. What's THIS?

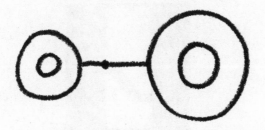

6. What's THIS?

7. What's THIS?

8. What's THIS?

9. What's THIS?

10. What's THIS?

11. What's THIS?

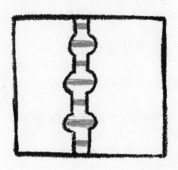

12. Here's a GRISLY one to end with.

What's THIS?

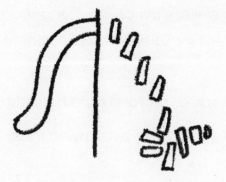

ANSWERS

1. A giraffe passing a first-floor window.

2. A bear climbing a tree.

3. Two worms falling in love.

4. A dachshund passing a gap in a fence.

5. An aerial view of a person in a sombrero frying an egg.

6. A spider performing the splits.

7. A mouse hiding behind a stone.

8. A snake on a zebra crossing.

9. An aerial view of another person in a different sombrero walking along a railway line.

10. A spider performing a handstand.

11. A snake after swallowing three tennis balls.

12. A worm climbing over a razor blade. (OUCH! At least there weren't any pictures of EGGS in this chapter.)

CHAPTER 19

THE 100 BEST (AND WORST) RIDDLES IN THE WORLD

SO HERE THEY ARE:

the **100 best** (and WORST)

riddles in the world.

A few of them are **fiendishly** clever,

a few of them are just very **silly**.

Some are very **OLD**,

some are brand NEW.

I hope **all** of them will have you

either SCRATCHING your head because

they're real **puzzlers** or exercising your

CHUCKLE muscles because they are so

ridiculous you've got to laugh.

And you can **eggspect** at least one

involving **eggs** –

it should CRACK you up! **ENJOY!**

1. As I was going to **St Ives**,

I met a man with seven **wives**,

Each wife had seven **sacks**,

Each sack had seven **cats**,

Each cat had seven **kits**.

Kits, cats, sacks and wives,

HOW MANY were there going to St Ives?

2. I'm tall when I'm young,

and I'm short when I'm old.

WHAT AM I?

3. Which **month** of the year has TWENTY-EIGHT days?

4. I am big on Saturday and Sunday.
I am small on Tuesday,
Wednesday and Thursday.
I am not on Monday and Friday.
What am I?

5. What does a **liar**
do when they **DIE**?

6. What is ALWAYS in front of you
but can't be **seen**?

7. What is hairy and FLIES?

8. George, Helen and Steve
are drinking **coffee**.
Dan, Karen and Dave
are drinking **water**.
Using **LOGIC**, and looking *carefully*
at their names, answer this question:
is **Ethel** drinking coffee *or* water?
And what about **Sam**?

9. There's a one-storey bungalow
in which **EVERYTHING** is **yellow**.
Yellow walls, **yellow** doors, **yellow** furniture.
What **COLOUR** are the stairs?

10. What can you **break**,
even if you **NEVER** pick it up or touch it?

11. You buy me **taken apart**,
To REDO what has been undone;
Four of my pieces have **one** sharp corner,
The rest of them have **none**.
WHAT AM I?

12. What **falls**, but does not BREAK,
and what **BREAKS** but does not **fall**?

13. I **shave** every day,
but my BEARD stays the same.
WHAT AM I?

14. You see a **boat** filled with people,
yet there isn't a SINGLE PERSON on board.
HOW is this possible?

15. On a **cold** night,
you walk into a DARK room
that contains a **match**,
a **candle**, a **stove** and an unlit **log fire**.
WHICH would you light first?

16. A man dies of OLD AGE on his **twenty-fifth** birthday. HOW is this possible?

17. I have **branches**, but no fruit, trunk or leaves. WHAT AM I?

18. What do you call a
very old **snowman**?

19. The **more** of this there is,
the less you see.
WHAT IS IT?

20. Tom's parents have **three** sons:
SNAP, **CRACKLE**, and
WHAT'S THE NAME of the third son?

21. I **follow** you all the time
and **copy** your every move,
but you can't TOUCH me or catch me.
WHAT AM I?

22. What has many **keys**
but can't OPEN a single lock?

23. What can you hold
in your **left** hand
but NOT in your **right**?

24. What do you get in **December**
that you DON'T get
in any OTHER month?

25. If a girl falls into a **well**,
why can't her BROTHER help her out?

26. I'm light as a **feather**, yet the STRONGEST person can't hold me for five minutes. **WHAT AM I?**

27. If you wanted to **wear** them, what would you call TWO BANANAS?

28. When is a **chair** like a piece of MATERIAL?

29. What do you call a **camel** with THREE humps?

30. If you've got me, you want to **share** me;

If you share me, you haven't **KEPT** me.

WHAT AM I?

31. What **can't** be

put in a SAUCEPAN?

32. Why are **robots**

never **AFRAID?**

33. If you're running in a race

and you **pass** the person

in SECOND place,

what place are **YOU** in?

34. What is **BLACK** and WHITE

and eats like a **horse?**

35. A boy met a girl who said,

'If I write your **exact weight**

on this piece of paper then you

will have to give me TEN POUNDS,

but if I can't I will pay YOU ten pounds.'

The boy looked around and saw no **scales**

or weighing machine, so he agreed,

thinking that WHATEVER the girl wrote

he'd just say he weighed a bit more or a bit less.

In the end, the boy ended up

paying the girl **ten pounds**.

HOW did the girl win the bet?

36. What has one **eye**

but can't SEE?

37. What has many **needles**
but doesn't SEW?

38. What has **hands**
but can't CLAP?

39. What has **legs**
but doesn't WALK?

40. If a BUTTERCUP is yellow,
what colour is a **hiccup**?

41. What can you **catch**
but not THROW?

42. Why is it **hard** to talk in front of a GOAT?

43. What has many **teeth** but can't BITE?

44. What has **words** but never SPEAKS?

45. What can **travel** all around the world without leaving its CORNER?

46. What has four LEGS and a TAIL and says '**Boo**'??

47. How can you make an **opera singer** out of TWO five-pound notes?

48. What is the smallest room?

49. What do you call a GIRL with a **radiator** on her head?

50. Where does ONE wall meet the OTHER wall?

51. Which building has the most **stories**?

52. What **tastes** better than it SMELLS?

53. What has thirteen **hearts** but NO other organs?

54. Which OLYMPIC **sport** is going DOWNHILL fast?

55. What kind of **coat** is best put on WET?

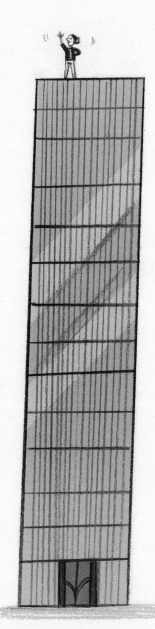

56. What has a **bottom** at the **top**?

57. What do you get when you cross a **CAT** with a PARROT?

58. What do you get when you cross a **cocker spaniel**, a POODLE and a COCKEREL?

59. What do you get if you cross a HEDGEHOG with a **GIRAFFE**?

60. What do **porcupines**
eat with their cheese?

61. Matilda has four **daughters**,
and each of her daughters
has one **brother**. HOW MANY children
does Matilda have?

62. Which is heavier:
a ton of **BRICKS** or a ton of FEATHERS?

63. Three **doctors** said
that Dan was their BROTHER.
Dan says he has **NO** brothers.
How many brothers does Dan *actually* have?

64. Two **FATHERS** and two SONS

are in a car, yet there are only

three people in the car.

HOW COME?

65. A clumsy boy goes to the shop

and buys a **dozen** eggs.

As he is going home, **ALL** but three break.

How many eggs are left UNBROKEN?

66. A man describes his sons, saying, 'They've all got **fair** hair, except for two of them; they've all got **brown** hair, except for two of them; they've all got **red** hair, except for two of them.' HOW MANY SONS does the man have?

67. If you have four ORANGES and a MELON in one hand and three LEMONS and two GRAPEFRUIT in the other hand, **what have you got**?

68. The day before **yesterday** I was eleven, and next year I will be FOURTEEN. WHEN is my birthday?

69. A girl has as many **BROTHERS** as SISTERS, but each brother has only **half** as many brothers as sisters. **HOW MANY** brothers and sisters are there in the family?

70. What **five-letter** word becomes shorter when you **ADD** two letters to it?

71. What do you get if you divide the CIRCUMFERENCE of a pumpkin by its **DIAMETER?**

72. A word I know, **six letters** it contains, Remove **ONE** letter and TWELVE remain. **WHAT IS IT?**

73. How do you know when you've **run** out of INVISIBLE INK?

74. You see me **ONCE** in June, TWICE in November and **not at all** in May. WHAT AM I?

75. TWO in a corner, one in a ROOM, **one** in a farm, but **none** in a flat or a house. WHAT IS IT?

76. I am the beginning of **everything**, the end of **everywhere**; I'm the beginning of **eternity**, the end of **time** and **space**. WHAT AM I?

77. What **four-letter** word can be written *forward*, backwards or upside down, and still be **READ** from left to right?

78. Forward I am **heavy**, but backwards I am NOT. **WHAT AM I?**

79. I am a word of letters **three**; add TWO and fewer there will be. **WHAT WORD AM I?**

80. What word of **five** letters has **one** left when two are REMOVED?

81. What comes at the **end** of every year?

82. Why did the **owl** 'owl?

83. What do you call the very tall buildings where **pigs** live?

84. What word is pronounced the **same** if you take away FOUR of its FIVE letters?

85. I am a **word** that begins with the letter 'I'. If you **ADD** the letter 'A' to me, I become a **new** word with a different meaning, but sound **exactly** the same. WHAT WORD AM I?

86. A man calls his **dog** from the opposite side of the river. The dog **crosses** the river without getting WET, and **without** using a bridge or boat. HOW?

87. What does a **duck** do when it flies UPSIDE DOWN?

88. If you **drop** me, I'm sure to crack,

But give me a **smile**

and I'll always smile back.

WHAT AM I?

89. I turn once,

what is **OUT** will not get IN.

I turn again, what is **IN** will not get OUT.

WHAT AM I?

90. What has **six legs**

and **HOWLS** at the moon?

91. I am always **hungry**

and will **DIE** if not fed,

but whatever I **touch**

will soon turn RED.

WHAT AM I?

92. What were three **nouns**, two **VERBS** and an ADJECTIVE doing in court?

93. What is small, red and **whispers** because it's got a sore throat?

94. What do you call an **insect** that bites and talks in CODE?

95. What do Winnie the Pooh and Alexander the Great have in **common**?

96. On a **cold night**, how FAR can you walk into the **WOODS**?

97. What can **jump** higher
than a BUILDING?

98. Horace and Doris Norris
were born on the **same** day
in the **same** year and are the
children of the **same** parents –
and yet they are NOT twins.
How come?

99. What's the **longest** word
in the English language?

100. What has to be **broken**
before you can USE it?

ANSWERS

1. *The traditional understanding of this rhyme is that only* **one** *is going to St Ives – the person telling the story. All of the others are coming from St Ives. The trick is that the listener assumes that all of the others must be added up, forgetting that only the storyteller says they are going to St Ives. If everyone mentioned in the riddle was bound for St Ives, then the number would be* **2,802**: *the storyteller, the man and his seven wives, forty-nine sacks, 343 cats and 2,401 kits.*

2. *A candle.*

3. *All of them.*

4. *The letter 'S'.*

5. *They lie still.*

6. *The future.*

7. *A hot-air baboon.*

8. *Ethel is drinking* **coffee**. *The letter 'E'*

appears twice in her name, as it does in the names of the others who are drinking coffee. Sam is drinking **water**. The letter 'A' appears once in his name, and the names of Dan, Karen and Dave, who are all drinking water too.

9. There aren't any stairs: it's a one-storey bungalow.

10. A promise.

11. A jigsaw puzzle.

12. **Night** falls and **day** breaks.

13. A barber.

14. All the people on the boat are married.

15. The match. (You need to light the match before you're able to light anything else!)

16. He was born on 29 February, so on his twenty-fifth birthday he will have lived one hundred years, because 28 February occurs in every year, but there is only a 29 February in every leap year.

17. A bank. (A bank with money can have different branches!)

18. *Water* – because he is so old he's melted!

19. Darkness.

20. Tom.

21. Your shadow.

22. A piano.

23. Your right elbow.

24. The letter 'D'.

25. Because he can't be a brother and assist her, too (**a sister**, too – get it?!).

26. Your breath.

27. A pair of slippers.

28. When it is satin.

29. Humphrey!

30. A secret.

31. Its lid.

32. Because they are made of metal and have nerves of steel.

33. Second place.

34. A zebra.

35. The girl did exactly what she said she would, and wrote '**your exact weight**' on the piece of paper.

36. A needle.

37. A Christmas tree.

38. A clock.

39. A table.

40. Burple!

41. A cold.

42. It always butts in.

43. A comb.

44. A book.

45. A stamp.

46. A cow with a cold.

47. Because two five-pound notes equal one tenor (**tenner**).

48. Mushroom.

49. Anita – as in a heater! (Remember, these are the **worst** as well as the best riddles in the world!)

50. On the corner.

51. The library.

52. A tongue.

53. A pack of cards.

54. Bobsleigh.

55. A coat of paint.

56. Legs.

57. A carrot.

58. A cockapoodledoo!

59. A ten-foot toothbrush.

60. Prickled onions.

61. Five – each daughter has the same brother.

62. Neither – they both weigh a ton.

63. None. He has three sisters.

64. The three are a grandfather, father and son.

65. Three.

66. Three: one with fair hair, one with brown hair and one with red hair.

67. Very big hands!

68. December 31 is my birthday; today is January 1. The day before yesterday I was eleven, so I turned twelve on my birthday, yesterday, December 31. I will be thirteen at the end of this year, on December 31, and then fourteen at the end of next year.

69. Four sisters and three brothers.

70. Short.

71. Pumpkin Pi.

72. Dozens.

73. It seems you can't see the answer . . .

74. *The letter 'E'.*

75. *The letter 'R'.*

76. *The letter 'E' again.*

77. *NOON.*

78. *The word 'ton'.*

79. *Few.*

80. *Stone. Take away 's' and 't' and 'one' is left. (And actually this is true for other words as well – phone, atone etc.!)*

81. *The letter 'R'.*

82. *Because the woodpecker would peck 'er!*

83. *Styscrapers.*

84. *Queue.*

85. *Isle – add an 'A' to make 'aisle'.*

86. *The river is frozen.*

87. *It quacks up!*

88. *A mirror.*

89. *A key.*

90. *A wolf. (I added two extra legs to make it harder. Tee-hee!)*

91. *Fire.*

92. *Waiting to be sentenced!*

93. *A hoarse radish.*

94. *A Morse-quito!*

95. *Their middle names!*

96. *On any night, you can only walk halfway into the woods. From then on, you are walking out of the woods!*

97. *Anything! Buildings can't jump.*

98. *Horace and Doris Norris are two children from a set of triplets. (The third triplet is called Maurice, but you probably guessed that.)*

99. *Smiles – because it has a mile between the first and last letters.*

100. *An egg – of course!*

THAT'S IT.

That's the *last* answer.

That's the *last* egg riddle.

It's time to make for the **eggsit**!

Yes, eggs have been a bit of a running joke,

haven't they? Or should that be a **runny yolk**?

And, speaking of jokes and eggs and yolks,

here's one *final* riddle to try out on a friend.

YOU: How do you spell the word 'joke'?

FRIEND: J, O, K, E.

YOU: How do you spell 'folk', as in 'folk music'?

FRIEND: F, O, L, K.

YOU: How do you spell the white of an egg?

FRIEND: Y, O, L, K.

YOU: No! No! No! You spell the white of an egg
like this: A, L, B, U, M, E, N. *Albumen* is the word
for the white of an egg. *Yolk* is the word for the
yellow of an egg.

GYLES BRANDRETH is the **WORLD'S** leading collector of **JOKES**.

He has also featured in the *Guinness Book of Records* for speaking **NON-STOP** for twelve and a half hours. He has appeared on **lots** of TV programmes, including *The One Show*, *Gogglebox*, *Pointless*, *Mastermind*, *Countdown*, *The Chase*, *Tipping Point*, *The IT Crowd*, *QI* and *Have I Got News for You*. On radio, he is a regular on *Just a Minute* and on stage he has appeared in **EVERYTHING** from Shakespeare to pantomime. Oh, yes, he has! (He once appeared in Shakespeare's most famous play, *Hamlet*. It was not a success. The audience threw **EGGS** at him. He went on as Hamlet; he came off as omelette.)

Once the Member of Parliament for the city of Chester, he is now chancellor of the University of Chester. As well as writing lots of books and collecting jokes and riddles, Gyles collects **TEDDY BEARS**. They all live in the Brandreth Bear House at Newby Hall, near Ripon in North Yorkshire.

Gyles lives in London with his wife, three children, seven grandchildren and the neighbour's cat, Nala.

Website: gylesbrandreth.net
Twitter: @GylesB1
Instagram: @gylesbrandreth

**Want more
from Master of Funny,
Gyles Brandreth?**

Discover the amazing joke
book that will make you laugh
yourself silly!

The BEST WORST Joke Book in the World!

What's **Black &
White & Red
ALL Over?**

MASTER OF FUNNY
Gyles Brandreth